D0938769

DATE DUE

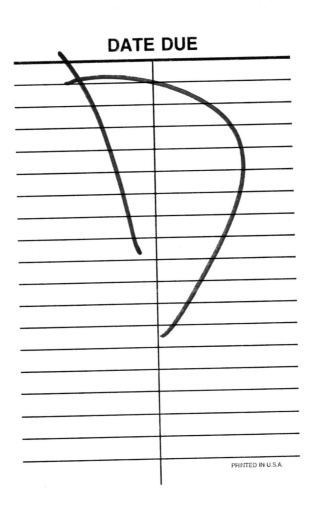

PRINTED IN U.S.A.

SPEED MACHINES

SPEEDBOATS

BY MATT SCHEFF

SportsZone

An Imprint of Abdo Publishing
www.abdopublishing.com

www.abdopublishing.com

Published by Abdo Publishing, a division of ABDO, PO Box 398166,
Minneapolis, Minnesota 55439. Copyright © 2015 by Abdo Consulting Group,
Inc. International copyrights reserved in all countries. No part of this
book may be reproduced in any form without written permission from the
publisher. SportsZone™ is a trademark and logo of Abdo Publishing.

Printed in the United States of America, North Mankato, Minnesota
092014
012015

Cover Photo: Felipe Dana/AP Images
Interior Photos: Felipe Dana/AP Images, 1, 26–27; Imaginechina via AP Images, 4–5,
24–25; Labrador Photo Video/Shutterstock Images, 6–7; Mazen Mahdi/Newscom, 7;
Hulton-Deutsch Collection/Corbis, 8–9; John Hacker, 10–11; Gary Stewart/AP Images,
12; AP Images, 12–13; Chuck Wagner/Shutterstock Images, 14–15; Shutterstock Images,
16, 18–19, 29; Darren Brode/Shutterstock Images, 16–17, 20–21, 31; Paul Lakatos/Zuma
Press/Newscom, 22–23; Florida Keys News Bureau, Andy Newman/AP Images, 28–29

Editor: Chrös McDougall
Series Designer: Nikki Farinella

Library of Congress Control Number: 2014944191

Cataloging-in-Publication Data
Scheff, Matt.
 Speedboats / Matt Scheff.
   p. cm. -- (Speed machines)
ISBN 978-1-62403-614-9 (lib. bdg.)
Includes bibliographical references and index.
1. Motorboats--Juvenile literature.   I. Title.
623.82--dc23
                                                                    2014944191

CONTENTS

F1 powerboats begin a race.

SPEED ON THE WATER

Drivers begin the final lap of the F1 powerboat race. The roars of 24 super-powerful V6 engines fill the air. Water sprays up behind the boats as they accelerate. The boats speed down a long, straight section of the course. They cruise over choppy waves. Soon, they approach the first turn.

FAST FACT

F1 powerboats can reach blistering speeds of more than 150 miles per hour (241 km/h)!

Powerboat racing legend Alex Carella is in second place. He dives hard into the turn, cutting inside the leader. Carella completes the pass and guns it down the final straightaway. He wins the race! Fans on shore cheer as the sport's greatest driver celebrates another victory.

Alex Carella (12) cruises to victory in an F1 powerboat race.

Alex Carella is one of the all-time great F1 powerboat drivers.

A motorboat cruises during a 1913 race in England.

SPEEDBOAT HISTORY

Nobody knows for sure when the first boat was invented. People have been using them for thousands of years. For most of that time, boats were powered by the wind, oars, or steam. All of that changed in 1886. That was when Germans Gottlieb Daimler and Wilhelm Maybach built the world's first gasoline-powered motorboat.

FAST FACT

The world's first motorboat race took place in 1903. Boats raced approximately 350 miles (563 km) across the English Channel.

The Kitty Hawk

The motorboat caught on fast. People built faster and faster boats. In 1911, US builder John Hacker built a motorboat called the Kitty Hawk. It could go an amazing 50 miles per hour (80 km/h). That made it one of the world's first speedboats.

People loved to race their speedboats, which were also called powerboats. In the 1960s, long ocean races were popular. One such competition was the Bahamas 500-mile (805-km) race. By the 1990s, most powerboat races were held on short courses of about 1 mile (1.6 km). That allowed fans to follow all of the action.

Dean Chenoweth races in a 1981 hydroplane race.

FAST FACT

Ultra-fast "superboats" first became popular during the 1980s. Many had three or more engines.

A hydroplane driver pulls away during a 1966 race in Maryland.

A powerboat is towed to the water at the 2012 offshore world championships.

THE PARTS OF A SPEEDBOAT

Today's speedboats come in different sizes and classes. But they all share the same basic parts. The main body of a boat is called the hull. A speedboat's hull is made of strong, lightweight materials, such as carbon fiber. Sometimes drivers decorate their hulls with artwork or sponsor logos.

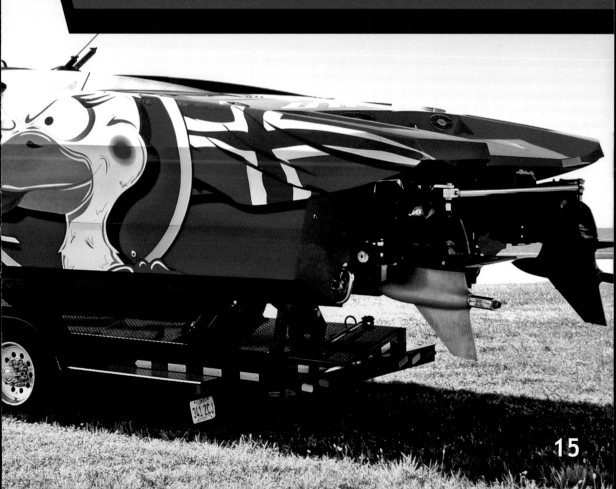

Jetboats are a type of speedboat with no propeller. Instead, they move by pumping a high-speed stream of water out of the back of the boat.

Outboard motors connect to the back of the boat.

Different speedboats use different ways to propel themselves. No matter the method, motors give speedboats their power. Outboard motors are attached to the back of a boat. Inboard motors are similar to car engines and are built into the boat. The fastest boats in the world are hydroplanes. Most boats plow through the water. Hydroplanes are ultra-fast speedboats that are built to skip over the surface of the water. Some of these boats use jet engines. These are the same type of engines used on jet airplanes!

A hydroplane cruises on the Detroit River in Michigan.

17

Most speedboat engines are connected to a set of spinning blades. Each blade is called a propeller or screw. As the blades spin, they push against the water. This forces the boat to go forward. The faster the propeller spins, the faster the speedboat goes.

A jetboat cruises the waters of New Zealand.

PHOTO DIAGRAM

1. Cockpit

2. Bow

3. Hull

4. Propeller/Screw

5. Motor

6. Stern

Two powerboats lose control
during a race.

SAFETY

Zooming over the waves at hundreds of miles per hour is highly dangerous. The fastest speedboats glide over the water. Too much speed or a wrong turn can cause them to rise up into the air and flip. That can be deadly for anyone in the boat.

Modern racing boats are designed for maximum driver safety.

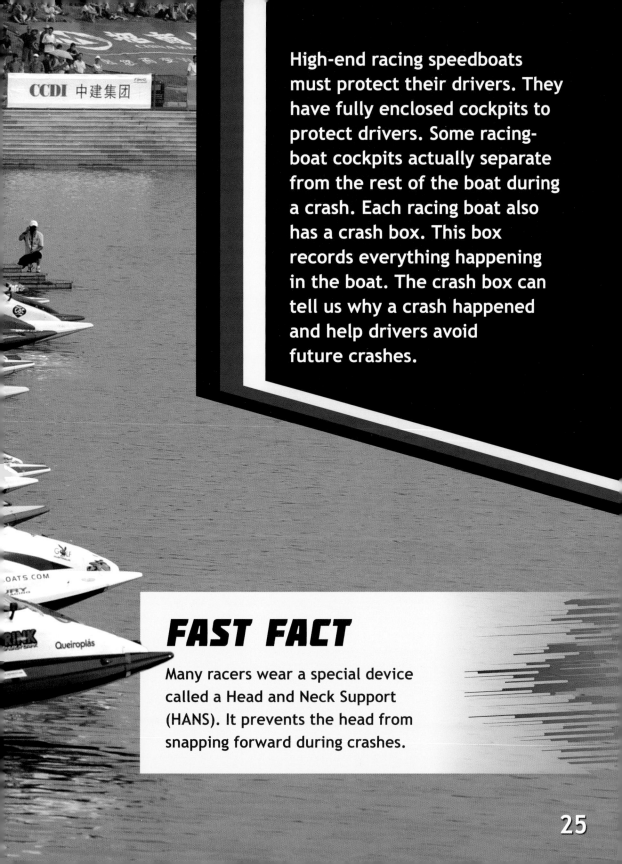

High-end racing speedboats must protect their drivers. They have fully enclosed cockpits to protect drivers. Some racing-boat cockpits actually separate from the rest of the boat during a crash. Each racing boat also has a crash box. This box records everything happening in the boat. The crash box can tell us why a crash happened and help drivers avoid future crashes.

FAST FACT

Many racers wear a special device called a Head and Neck Support (HANS). It prevents the head from snapping forward during crashes.

COMPETITION

There are dozens of different types of speedboat races. But they fall into two main categories: offshore and inshore. Offshore races take place in the open ocean. Inshore races are held in an enclosed body of water, such as a lake.

The Class 1 World Powerboat Championship is the biggest offshore racing series. Custom-built racing boats compete in point-to-point races that stretch hundreds of miles.

FAST FACT

The most coveted trophy in hydroplane racing is called the Gold Cup.

Two powerboats race in the United Arab Emirates.

Inshore races take place on short courses. The F1 Powerboat (F1H2O) World Championship is the biggest inshore racing series. It has races all over the world. These races last for dozens of laps over a span of 30 minutes. Then the racers charge through two additional laps to determine the winner. Racers earn points for their finishes in each race. The racer with the most points at the end is the F1H2O champion.

Powerboats race in Key West, Florida.

A powerboat races at the F1H2O
World Championship.

GLOSSARY

accelerate
To gain speed.

carbon fiber
A strong, lightweight material used to make some speedboat hulls.

cockpit
The enclosed area in which a pilot or driver sits.

hull
The main body of a boat or ship.

hydroplane
The fastest type of speedboat; hydroplanes are designed to glide over the surface of the water.

inboard motor
A type of motor built into the back of a boat, similar to a car's engine.

jet engine
A type of engine that produces power by forcing air or water out at high speeds.

outboard motor
A type of motor that is attached to the back of a boat.

point-to-point race
A race in which speedboats race from one location to another, rather than completing laps on a set course.

propeller
A set of rapidly spinning blades that push a boat into motion.

sponsor
A company or person that supports a driver, often by providing money. In return, the driver promotes the company or person.

FOR MORE INFORMATION

Books
Graham, Ian. *Speedboats—And Other Fast Machines in the Water*. Irvine, CA: QEB Publishing, 2010.

Tieck, Sarah. *Speedboats*. Edina, MN: Abdo Publishing Co., 2010.

Websites
To learn more about Speed Machines, visit **booklinks.abdopublishing.com.** These links are routinely monitored and updated to provide the most current information available.

INDEX

ABOUT THE AUTHOR

Matt Scheff is a freelance author and lifelong motor sports fan living in Minnesota.